THE CRICKET-BAT;

AND

HOW TO USE IT:

A TREATISE ON

THE GAME OF CRICKET.

WITH PRACTICAL AND SCIENTIFIC INSTRUCTIONS
IN BATTING, BOWLING, AND FIELDING:

The Laws of Cricket,

MATCH-PLAYING, SINGLE-WICKET, &c.

BY

AN OLD CRICKETER.

1861.

PREFACE.

THOUGH Cricketing is one of the most popular
games of the present age, there are fewer works
of authority upon the subject than upon any
other of our English recreations. The Author,
therefore, ventures to hope, that in sending
forth this little volume (the result of long and
devoted experience), it may be found worthy of
a place in the ranks of approved treatises on the
National Sports and Pastimes of England.

London, 1861.

CONTENTS.

THE CRICKET-BAT;

AND HOW TO USE IT.

THE HISTORY OF THE GAME OF CRICKET.

"Lo! cricketing its fame extends like raylines from the sun,
If the round world has claim to ends, thither its courses run;
The stumps are raised far off and wide, the sound from bat
    and ball
Is heard where runs the lava tide and roaring waters fall."
Song of the Cricketer.

THE origin of the game, with the derivation of
the word "Cricket," cannot be satisfactorily
traced; and the name of the originator has
hitherto remained undiscovered; which is the
more extraordinary when considered that cricket
is by no means an ancient game.   No allusion
is made to it by ancient writers, nor do any of
the early poets make use of the word.   Shake-
speare is also silent upon the subject, though, as

B

every reader knows, there are constant references in the works·of the immortal bard to all the then known diversions of man. Other dramatists of the same age being also silent on the subject, and the result of other researches tending to the same conclusion, we are induced to believe there is no authentic trace of the game until the year 1702; about which date it is supposed to have been first· known and practised. Strutt and Junius have both attempted to trace the word to the Saxon tongue, but upon very meagre and unsatisfactory authority ; and, as is believed, erroneously endeavouring to give the ancients the credit of inventing the game.

The Rev. J. Pycroft, in a modern work called " The Cricket Field," attempts to make out that the ancient game of *club-ball* was the original and identical game of cricket; and that club-ball was the old name for cricket. But the evidence adduced in support of his argument, is by no means clear or satisfactory. Club-ball is well known as a very ancient game, and totally distinct from that of cricket. And there is no trace of any alteration in the game of " club-ball," nor of any substitution to that of " cricket."

Antiquarians one and all have been unable to

trace it beyond the date above quoted. One fact, however, is pretty certain—its birth is purely English. If the game had been known to the ancients, it is impossible to imagine that no record or mention of it would have been found. The athlete of old delighted and excelled in manly games, and even encouraged them with almost equal ardour to the pursuits of study. It may therefore be fairly supposed that this game (if known to them) would have been highly popular ; and there would be found traces of it among those of other games.

Strutt, in his " Sports and Pastimes," says, he can find no record of the game, under its present appellation, beyond the period of the commencement of the last century. Nyren* has a strong opinion that the game originated with the Saxons, and thinks the derivation of the word is probably from the Saxon "cpyce," a stick. He also adds in support of his opinion, that " those who are acquainted with some of the remote and unfrequented villages of England, where the primitive manners, customs, and games of our ancestors survive in the perfection

* One of the earliest and most celebrated cricketers, and author of " *The Cricketer's Tutor*."

of rude and unadulterated simplicity, must have remarked the lads playing at a game, which is the same in its outline and principal features as the consummate piece of perfection that at this day is the glory of Lords, and the pride of English athlete. I mean the one in which a single stick is appointed for a cricket; ditto for a bat; and the same repeated of about three inches in length for a ball. If this be not the original of the game of cricket, it is a plebeian imitation of it."

It is not disputed that the game alluded to by Nyren is one which in its outline bears some resemblance to cricket: but is not this the game of " club-ball," or " cat," or some such game, still played under its. original name? What trace is there to connect it with cricket? And if, on the other hand, it is neither ".club-ball," nor " cat," then, it may be said there is.nothing to shew that the game alluded to by Nyren as played by " the lads of the village" is of more ancient origin than the game of cricket: on the contrary, it may be of subsequent origin to that of cricket.

Upon reference to the best standard works upon the subject, the results of researches by those who have written upon cricket, shows, that no satisfactory trace of the game can be discovered anterior to the year 1702 : and the derivation of the word has never been made out ; nor is there anything to prove that the game was ever known by any other name than that of " cricket."

From these, the earliest traces, it appears that the wickets originally employed were only one foot in height; but pitched from two to three feet in width.

Anciently, the game was played in this manner :—a hole was cut in the ground between the stumps and the popping-crease; this hole was large enough to admit the ball and but-end of the bat; and, on running from one wicket to the other, the batsman had to strike the lower end of his bat into the hole, in order to score. By the modern practice the batsman has merely to touch the ground over the popping-crease ; the hole being entirely done away with.

And according to the ancient game, there were no bails: the wicket-keeper instead of touching the wicket and knocking off the bail, had to put the ball into the hole alluded to, in order to put out the batsman. The consequence was, that whenever a run took place, the wicket-keeper was in the greatest danger, and seldom escaped without getting his hands severely bruised by the batsman in his eagerness to save the run, by thrusting his bat into the hole, regardless of all consequences to the hands and arms of the wicket-keeper. The dangerous nature of this scramble as to whether the bat or the ball should be first in the hole, ultimately led to a suggestion for some alteration in regard to the mode of putting out the striker; and the invention of bails was introduced, together with a rule, that in absence of bails, the act of putting down the wicket should be tantamount to putting the ball in the hole. About the same period as this wholesome alteration took place, the wickets were raised to the height of 22 inches, and their breadth considerably contracted.

Most of the subsequent important alterations in the game, were made during the time of that celebrated cricketer, already alluded to—John Nyren. There were two Nyrens, John and Richard, both famous cricketers: the distinguished man, John, was born in or about the year 1764: he was termed the "father and general " of the celebrated old Hambledon Club: he was also a distinguished player in the Marylebone Club.

It also appears that, in the game, as originally played, it was not usual to *block* the ball, but to strike every time it came within reach. The original bat was ill adapted for the purposes of blocking or defending the wicket, otherwise than by striking; it being not unlike, in shape, a table-knife with a curve in the back.

According to Nyren, the present form of the cricket-bat was not adopted till the year 1746; and he alludes to a match played in that year with the old-fashioned bat. The match referred to arose out of a challenge given by the then Lord Sackville, on behalf of the County of Kent, to play against All England. This, it appears, was a very spirited and well contested match: but Nyren says—

" The hitting however, could neither have been of a high character, nor indeed safe, as may be gathered from the figure of the bat at that time; which was similar to an *old-fashioned dinner-knife, curved at the back, and sweeping in the form of a volute at the front and end !* With such a bat, the system must have been all for hitting; it would be barely possible to block: and when the practice of bowling length balls was introduced, and which gave the bowler so great an advantage in the game, it became absolutely necessary to change the form of the bat, in order that the striker might be able to keep pace with the improvement. It was therefore made straight in the pod; in consequence of which, a total revolution—it may be said a reformation too— ensued in the style of play."

After the fashion of the bat had been altered into a straight form, the system of blocking the ball became a general mode of defensive play among all cricketers.

But, although "straight in the pod," the bat was still very wide; and when the blocking system became popular, and batsmen found, that with ordinary skill, they could keep their places at the wickets a long time, the form of the bats gradually grew wider; and as there was no law in those days restricting the bat to any particular width; many cricketers came to the wickets with bats as broad as scavengers' shovels.

This state of things could not last long; and

it became absolutely necessary to frame a stringent rule as to the extreme width of the bat. This rule was made in Nyren's time, as will appear from the following quotation from his able little book.

"Several years since (I do not recollect the precise date) a player, named White, of Ryegate, brought a bat to a match, which, *being the width of the stumps*, effectually defended his wicket from the bowler: and in consequence, a law was passed limiting the future width of the bat to 4¼ inches."

Nyren adds, "I have a perfect recollection of this occurence; and, that, subsequently, an iron frame of the *statute* width, was constructed for, and kept by, the Hambledon Club; through which any bat of suspected dimensions was passed, and allowed or rejected accordingly."

It appears that up to the year 1775, the wicket comprised two stumps only. The addition of the third stump arose out of a memorable match played on the 22nd of May in that year, on the Artillery Ground, at Finsbury, between five of the Hambledon Club and five of All England.

Nyren says of this match—" Lumpy * was
bowler upon the occasion ; and it having been
remarked that his balls had three several times
passed between Small's † stumps, it was considered to be a hard thing upon the bowler that
his straightest balls should be thus sacrificed ;
the number of stumps was, in consequence
increased from two to three. Many amateurs
were of opinion at the time, that the alteration
would tend to shorten the game : and subsequently the Hampshire gentlemen did me the
honour of taking my opinion upon this point.
I agreed with them that it was but doing
justice to the bowler ; but I differed upon the
question that it would shorten the game ;
because the striker, knowing the danger of
missing one straight ball, with three instead of
two stumps behind him, would naturally re-
double his care ; while every loose, hard hitter
would learn to stop, and play as safe a game as
possible."

Such is the origin of the *three* stumps which
have ever since formed the wicket.

* A celebrated bowler of that name.
† Small was also a famous cricketer of that time.

MODERN PROGRESS OF THE GAME.

THOUGH of comparatively modern origin, cricket seems to have taken precedence of all other national games. Indeed, the boundless and increasing popularity of the game places it far in advance of all other recreations of the people. The numbers of names enrolled as members of cricket clubs at the present day, are beyond all precedent. No other national sport is so extensively indulged in, or so universally practised by all ranks and grades of society.

There can be no more convincing proof of the popularity of the game, than that of the immense and increasing support it receives at the hands of every class of the community: princes, peers, commoners, judges, barristers, doctors of law, physic, and divinity; clergymen, surgeons, attorneys, soldiers, sailors, farmers, tailors; and indeed members of every profession, every trade, and every denomination are more or less cricketers.

" The vassal and peer in the pastime engage— ,
   The hale mountain peasant—the chief in the glen;
   All ages commingle—youth, warrior, and sage,
   For of men it makes boys, and boys it makes men."

To soldiers especially, cricket has many charms, and is of essential service, not only in the developement of muscular activity and vigour, but also in the promotion of good feeling in the ranks; with contentment and health.

It is the chosen recreation of the soldier during weary campaigns; the delight of every British tar when he obtains a "liberty day" to run ashore—

" Old ocean's chiefs, who dangers brave,
   Join him with horny hand;
   And statesmen here, distinctions waive,
   Though magnates of the land."

Indeed my pen only fails me when I endeavour to find a class with whom the game is in disfavour.

Though by no means an ancient game, it has risen by rapid and gigantic strides to the highest pinnacle of popularity, as a manly, healthful, and useful recreation. Those persons whose daily occupations are sedentary, find it pecu-

liarly advantageous to health, to devote a few
hours to the game; though in some cases only
once or twice a week. The game has, for years
past, ranked as one of the most prominent in
the catalogue of manly and scientific sports;
and, judging from past and present experiences,
there will be no flagging: but the same current
of popular favour which now bears it along,
foremost in the van, will not cease to flow so
long as England remains supreme, and continues
to produce stalwart and athletic sons.

No game tends more to the developement of
muscular strength and activity than cricket;
and whilst it is encouraged and practised with
that spirit and enthusiasm which prevails at
present, there will be no degeneration in muscular strength, activity, and vigour, in the sons
of old England, nor in the ranks of British
soldiers.

The youth who has been trained in the
cricket-field will be the more easily trained for
the army; he will make the better soldier, the
more active swordsman; and the better dis-
ciplined and more nimble sailor, than he who
is totally unacquainted with manly and athletic
exercises.

The late Duke of Wellington once remarked
in the House of Lords, that his success in arms
was owing, in a great measure, to the manly
sports of Great Britain, in which, in his youthful
days, he said he freely indulged; and one sport
above all—cricket.   Others of our best-disci-
plined and bravest soldiers and sailors have
made similar assertions.

It is, therefore, of vast national importance
that encouragement should be given, and favour
shown towards this widely-popular diversion.

Physical recreations were always regarded by
the ancients as of the highest importance in the
training of youth; and were encouraged in
nearly equal proportion with the exercise of the
mind; because it was found that nothing
tended more successfully to keep both body and
mind in a healthful state than a combination or
equalization of the two—one being evidently in
a measure dependent on the other; for, without
health of body, the mind could not be in a fit
state for study.   A consistent indulgence in
athletic sports has therefore, from the days of
the Greeks and Romans, down to the present
time, always formed part of the training and
education of youth.

No nation in the world can vie with us in the perfection and extent to which we carry our national sports ; and with no people is the game of cricket so eagerly indulged in as by the English. The joys of the cricket-field extend from shore to shore ; they have attained a world-wide fame ; and in every land, and at every port, no matter how far distant from our shores, if there be a few Englishmen in the place, they will insist on their dear old game of cricket.

Cricket now ranks so highly as a scientific game, that, to become a thorough proficient, a man must have devoted much time and attention to the pursuit, with many years' practical experience. In former days there were no "professionals," but now it would be almost impossible to do without them : and there is no doubt that a few hours' practice with a professional cricketer does more towards improving a tyro than months of practice among self-taught players. The services of a man who has made cricket his profession, cannot be too highly appreciated by aspiring cricketers.

The members of all country cricket-clubs, who aim at distinction, engage one or more professional players or bowlers to assist and instruct them throughout the season : and the benefit those members derive from such instruction, is frequently acknowledged and followed by marked improvement; and often, ultimate distinction. At the present day there are so many eminent professionals, that no difficulty is found in securing efficient services whenever required.

By the rules of almost every club, swearing and profane language are forbidden on pain of fine ; and, for a second offence, in some clubs, expulsion. This is a most wholesome regulation, and should be conspicuously placarded in every cricket-room; nothing tends so much to good example by the higher classes as a strict observance of this rule ; whilst nothing is more derogatory to the players, and injurious to the purity of the game, than a disregard of it.

In a pecuniary point of view, cricket may be enjoyed at the least expense of any game ; and though there are ways and means of making it as luxurious and extravagant as the most princely diversion, it may be brought within the measure of the most humble. Indeed, it is the cheapest amusement that can be had ; and there is none which so deservedly possesses that unbounded popularity to which it has, within a few years past, so rapidly ascended.

> " Then welcome the sober enjoyment that flings,
>   Such witchery round the spot where it lives !
> The bud in the heart, to the sunlight that clings,
>   Will bloom in the pleasure that cricketing gives."

When the sons of old England are all driven from their native land by foreign foes, then— and not till then—will the bat, the ball, and the wicket be laid aside and forgotten : but so long as British sports and manly exercises are prac- tised and encouraged, there will be no deteriora- tion in strength, activity, and courage among the defenders of our land : and foremost in the *ranks*, in the event of war or invasion, among those who are most skilful in the use of warlike weapons, will be the boys who in earlier days were most skilled in the use of the cricket-bat.

CRICKETING QUALIFICATIONS.

AMONG the most essential qualifications of a cricketer are activity of body, good eyesight, mus- cular strength, and precision in the use of hand. The first of these, activity of body, is an indis- pensable quality : a slothful or inactive fellow

C

will never make a good cricketer. A quick
and watchful eye, with long sight, is also
highly essential: a short-sighted man cannot
play properly at the game without spectacles ;
and to say nothing of the danger of wearing
such artificial contrivances in the cricket-field,
they are otherwise so inconvenient that no
short-sighted person should incur the risk of
cricketing either with or without spectacles.
At every stroke of the arm, or other sudden or
violent movement, spectacles are apt to fly off, or
shift their position from the bridge of the nose
to the upper lip of the wearer ; and after much
running or excitement, the heat of the face
makes them cloudy and obscure ; so that a
short-sighted cricketer is never to be depended·
on ; neither can he always depend on his own
skill, though long practised.   Such are the
misfortunes of short sight.   The precision of
the eye and hand, acting conjointly, are of the
essence of the art of bowling, batting, blocking,
and catching.

Great muscular strength may sometimes tell
very forcibly in batting and bowling, still it is
not an essential qualification ; for it has often
been proved, that skill and art display supe-

riority over great strength of arm. Art is therefore, in most instances, preferable to great muscular strength; but the two combined, in a good cricketer, render him a formidable opponent, both as a bowler and batter.

A nervous man never makes a good cricketer: when the game is critical such a man is always very soon out at the wicket. A shrewd or "wide awake" fellow makes the distinguished cricketer, not the dull and stupid one.

To play a game of cricket, twenty-six persons are required: viz., twenty-two players, two umpires, and two scorers.

Although the game is usually played with eleven on each side, there is no restriction as to numbers; the parties may stipulate for eleven v. twenty-two, twelve v. twenty, twenty v. sixteen, &c. &c.

The ground must be smooth; it should be well rolled and watered in dry weather, the grass being previously fed down by sheep.

THE CRICKETER'S DRESS.

IT is only necessary to say as to the dress of the cricketer, that regard should always be had to materials which absorb perspiration ; and, in sultry weather, there is nothing so safe and comfortable as a thin woollen shirt.

Never wear silk, when taking active exercise : it is a dangerous material, being a nonconductor of heat.

Wear trowsers made of flannel ; the material to be well shrunk before being made up. The socks should be of thin woollen material.

Attention to these apparently trivial matters is the means of preserving your health, and increasing your enjoyment of the game. Freedom of limb being highly essential to the performance of active exercises, braces, straps, and bandages should be discarded.

Spikes in the shoes are sometimes indispensable : they should not be put in until after the shoe has been worn and the foot becomes accustomed to it.

THE BAT;

AND HOW TO HANDLE IT.

In order to use the bat with greatest effect, the striker or batsman must be thoroughly familiar with the best mode of handling it.

If you stand at the wicket in a careless position, hold the bat wrong, or are otherwise negligent or awkward, you can neither strike with precision nor block with certainty.

Take hold of the bat with both hands in the middle of the handle; the palm of the right hand being turned *from* the body, and the palm of the left *towards* the body: place the hands near to each other, but not touching. Bear in mind that if the hands are far apart the batsman will have far less control over the bat than if close together: and besides too, he will not be able to hit so hard, nor stop a ball so effectively, when the hands are wide apart.

When standing at the wicket in expectation of a ball, and when blocking or striking at straight balls, always keep the face of the bat perfectly square, and fronting the opposite wicket.

And the young cricketer must remember, that in order to play safely and effectively at a length or leaping ball which comes straight, he will have to turn up and bend his left elbow: this is a very important rudimentary principle ; and one which should be strictly adhered to by all aspiring cricketers on first handling the bat ; because, in the event of hitting or stopping balls, with the bat upright or lifted, if the left elbow be raised as suggested, the batsman has quicker action and double power over the ball ; added to which, it will not rise.

For the purposes of blocking, the hands may be held a *little* apart with advantage : but for all purposes of striking they should be close together.

RUDIMENTARY LESSONS

ON THE USE OF THE CRICKET-BAT.

" Twas in the prime of summer time,
   An evening calm and cool,
And five-and-twenty happy boys
   Came bounding out of school:
Away they sped with gamesome minds,
   And souls untouched with sin ;
To a level mead they came, and there
   They drove the wickets in."

                  HOOD.

BEGINNERS should first look on and learn the position and duties of every man in the field : a great deal of cricket is to be learnt from example.

They should then commence by practising all the different performances, to *slow* bowling: and be sure to pay the greatest attention to their fielding ; as that is of more importance to a young cricketer than anything.

The tyro should bear in mind that inattention and inexperience are generally the cause of danger and accidents in the cricket-field.

Directions have already been given, under the preceding head, as to the mode of holding and handling the bat. When at the wicket, stand as near the front of the wicket as you can, without standing before it. Stand easy, and hold the bat lightly ; do not clench it firmly until the moment before using it. In running between the wickets carry your bat in the right hand ; and always run to the right : your fellow batsman doing the same, awkward collisions will thus be avoided.

There is much for the tyro to learn in his rudimentary instructions as to the pitch of the balls : he must watch attentively, and in course of time he will know whether or not it is safe to strike ; or whether it would not be more prudent to block. A good deal of judgment and practice is required as to this.

The best mode of instruction that can be recommended, is, a few good practical lessons from an experienced player : if he will take the necessary pains in teaching you, improvement is sure to follow.

Always play on the top of the ball, and hit it slantwise, towards the ground.

Meet the ball with the bat full-faced. Never

allow the ball to strike the bat; such is bad
and careless play, and is termed *hanging guard*.
In every instance take care that by the movements of the wrist and muscles you *play the
bat at the ball:* and this rudimentary principle
applies especially to blocking.

Play with coolness and decision; particularly
when striking; you will hit so much the harder,
more surely, and correctly.

A nervous or timid hitter never makes a good
cricketer.

Do not attempt to play with a heavy bat:
select one that you can use as if it were a mere
whip in your hands; and easy and comfortable
to feel.

Always be careful to keep your position behind the popping-crease: and take care not to get
into the habit of running in to strike. Many a
promising young cricketer has become an un-
steady and unsafe player, through once acquiring the habit of advancing to strike.
Liberties of the kind may sometimes be taken
with advantage, by cricketers of long experience,
but not by tyros. It may be, that "forward
play" (as it is termed) by well facing the ball,
is the more graceful, and most admired style;

and perhaps easier learned than back play : the latter, however, often runs up the score rapidly.

Fix your eyes intently on the bowler, and look sharp for the ball as it leaves his hands.

Commence your innings by striving to keep your place, and endeavouring to obtain single runs ; you will then become used to the bowler and his style.

Always remember, in striking, that if you miss the ball, it will probably hit the wicket : for, though it may come a little wide, still it may, by a very slight swerve, twist or plunge into the wicket.

It is very necessary for a young cricketer to acquire a mode of using the bat in a perpendicular manner, when striking or guarding the wicket.

When the ball is apparently coming straight to the wicket, of course the only safe mode of guarding is, either to block, or strike with the bat in a perpendicular position, and slightly leaning towards or over the ball : and the same rule should be observed when the ball is a little wide, either on the off or near side.

Horizontal play at a straight ball is very bad play ; indeed, the most unsafe of all.

When the pitch or course of the ball is such as to preclude all danger of its hitting the wicket, the batsman should strike boldly; being careful not to hit the ball so that it flies up in the air.

Never strike too hard or beyond your strength, lest you overbalance yourself, and miss the ball altogether.

The face of the bat should always be held square to the wicket; or, rather, broadside on, at straight balls: but at wide or deviating ones, the face of the bat may be slightly turned. And for the purpose of blocking a very swift ball, this slight turn, when judiciously performed, is sometimes the means of obtaining two or three runs.

All the difficult performances in the game of cricket must be learnt off slow-bowling: and as you improve, the bowler should gradually increase the rate and advance the style of bowling.

By reaching in after a wide ball, a young player seldom hits it, he strikes under it; and if he happens to hit it, gives a chance to the fieldsmen of catching him out.

When a *length ball* is pitched a little wide of

the off stump, the young cricketer had better leave it alone, particularly if he is short in stature : by playing at it he will do no good ; he could scarcely play it with safety, and if he did, he would probably get no run.

Experienced batsmen are always wary of playing at these balls : though with good judgment, a man of tall stature or long limbs may sometimes play it safely, by directing its course between middle wicket and point, and so obtain a run.

Be careful in making a leg-hit : it is one of those hits over which the striker has less control than over others. He should step back a little when it comes inside or close to the leg-stump ; and when it comes wide of it, he should step quickly in front, turn, and hit it. This mode of play, however, will be fully explained in the finishing lessons : the tyro should not venture too soon on attempting it.

Straight balls, when slowly bowled and pitched a length, the young batter may, if he has confidence, go in at, and strike boldly ; being careful to play with his bat held perpendicularly.

If the ball comes wide of the wicket, he cannot play with the bat upright, unless he moves out of his proper position.

There can be no certainty in a tyro's hitting the ball, unless he plays with the bat held perpendicularly. And if he stands with his legs too wide apart, or too close, he cannot make either a good or safe hit.

BLOCKING.

THE young batsman should pay particular attention to the art of blocking, or stopping a ball. Indeed he cannot devote too much time or trouble to learning thoroughly the art: it is one of the greatest accomplishments in the use of the cricket-bat; and one which alone enables a man, at all times, to cut a formidable figure at the wicket; and become a troublesome opponent to the bowler.

The mode of blocking straight balls is easily learnt, with attention. As already stated, when you are standing at the wicket, just before the bowler delivers the ball, you raise the bat: when it is a "length ball" and comes straight, and for fear of missing it if you strike, or not having sufficient confidence or certainty of

hitting, you prefer blocking, step forward a full
stride, with the *left foot only ;* taking especial
care to *keep the right foot behind the popping-
crease :* hold the bat firmly, presenting its full
broad face to the opposite wicket : but do not
hold the bat quite upright ; slant it from the
top of the handle to an angle of about twenty or
twenty-two degrees ; the upper part of the bat
inclining towards the opposite wicket.

This mode of *reaching* in for the purpose of
blocking a *length ball* must be practised and
thoroughly learnt by all aspiring batsmen. It
is the means by which you not only prevent the
ball hitting the wicket, but also stop it from
rising or twisting. The slant of the bat pre-
vents the ball from rising ; whereas, if the bat
were held upright, the ball would fly up and give
the fieldsmen a chance of catching you out.

If, in blocking, you are careless, and advance
the right foot from behind the popping-crease,
and happen to miss the ball, if the wicket-
keeper is attending to his duties, he will instantly stump you out.

Although the art of blocking must be well
learnt, the young cricketer must take care not
to acquire a timid mode of play, and block every

ball that is pitched to him. He should cut
and strike boldly at loose balls, and block those
only which are critical and dangerous to his
wicket.

Pycroft says, in "The Cricket-Field:"—

"Mere stopping balls and poking about in the
block-hole is not cricket, however successful:
and I must admit that I once saw one of the
most awkward, poking vexatious blockers that
ever produced a counterfeit of cricket, defy
Bayley and Cobbett at Oxford, three hours, and
make five-and-thirty runs! Another friend, a
better player, addicted to the same teasing game,
in a match at Exeter in 1845, blocked away till
his party, the N. Devon, won the match, chiefly
by byes and wide balls! Such men might have
turned their powers to much better account."

In guarding the wicket, remember that on
*any little deviation from the very centre of
the block*, the ball is into your wicket in an
instant. The leg-stump is the one most frequently hit.

CATCHING OUT THE STRIKER.

THIS performance is always a subject of con-
gratulation to the fieldsman who does it well :
and a matter of rejoicing to the adversaries of
a troublesome batsman. On the other hand it
is always a matter of annoyance to the whole
field when one of the party fails in a fair catch,
or performs it in a bungling or "butter-
fingered" style. But although a matter of
annoyance to the whole field when an easy
catch is missed, it is great glee to the batsman,
who is then enabled to continue his place at the
wicket.

In attempting to catch a ball, keep the eye
steadily fixed upon it; the hands elevated as
high as the chest or rather higher ; the wrists
close, hands and fingers open and ready to
clasp and receive the ball into the palms of the
hands; closing the fingers as it comes, and
yielding to the jerk with the arms alone.

Learn also, by frequent practice, to catch the
ball with either hand, singly.

STUMPING OUT.

THIS performance is done either by the wicket-keeper or the bowler. It is that by which the striker is put out, and loses his place at the wicket, through moving away from it when the ball is in play, though in the hands of the bowler or wicket-keeper; either of whom can put the striker out by knocking off a bail with the ball, at a moment when he has moved away with his bat beyond the popping-crease.

BOWLING.

THE art of bowling is one of the most important and brilliant qualifications in good cricketing. There are some men who are never able to bowl well, though they practise it long and frequently : whilst there are others who excel in it very early in their practice.

A few years ago there were no less than four different styles of bowling, which were sanctioned at most of the matches played in England: viz.—

1. Under-hand bowling.
2. Over-hand or round-arm bowling

D

3. The jerking style.

4. The throwing style.

Under-hand bowling is the oldest of all, and indeed the only legitimate style: all innovations and deviations from it are more or less objectionable.

Round-arm or *over-hand bowling.*—Had this objectionable style of bowling been nipped in the bud, as it deserved, very much controversy and ill feeling would have been avoided: but it was allowed at the time of its birth, as if an improvement: and probably in its least objectionable style it was so; but it was the indirect means of introducing the two other highly unfair styles of *jerking* and *throwing*. One system led on to the other: a slight jerk was added to the round-arm style, followed by a bold and more determined jerk; and eventually the system of round-arm bowling positively assumed a form of *throwing* or hurling the ball: so that from the hands of a powerful man, of strong muscular frame, the ball came towards the wickets like a shot from an artillery field-piece: and from that time, the game of cricket became one of extreme danger. Tom Walker, a cricketer of Nyren's time, is the man who first introduced the objectionable system of throwing the ball. The balls so thrown or hurled, came with sufficient force to inflict severe and dangerous wounds among those behind the wickets. And if the ground happened to be a little uneven the danger was considerably increased, because of the uncertain course and deviation of the ball.

Felix,* in discussing the system of round-arm bowling, says—"We can only now add, that we regret that this innovation should ever have been allowed to come into action; not because it has not been met with excellent, good tempered, and well practised skill, but because it has introduced so many new kinds of chances, all aiming at the destruction and annoyance of the batsman, to say nothing of the increased danger which must ever exist upon grounds that are not smooth."

Felix was always opposed to round-arm bowling: he speaks of it as a "reckless invention," adding, that underhand-bowling was always considered, and has of late years been proved to be "sufficiently efficacious for all purposes of the game."

* Felix "On the Bat."

The objectionable system rendered necessary leather casings, military gauntlets, india-rubber paddings, and cork and whalebone accoutrements of various descriptions.

The old law of the Marylebone Club Rules, as revised in 1830, stood thus—

" The ball shall be bowled. If it be thrown or jerked, or if any part of the hand or arm be above the shoulder at the time of delivering, the umpire shall call ' no ball!'"

According to the latest alteration (1860) the law of the Marylebone Club stands thus—

" The ball must be bowled. If thrown or jerked, or if the bowler in the actual delivery of the ball, or in the action *immediately preceding the delivery*, shall raise his hand or arm above his shoulder, the umpire shall call ' no ball!'"

The system of throwing the ball, instead of bowling it, has therefore very properly been forbidden by the above special rule of the Marylebone Club; and indeed every cricket-club would do well to follow that example. Round-arm bowling is all very well when performed without hurling the ball, starting it with a jerk, or delivering it above the elbow. The

practice of throwing the ball, though only so
recently abolished as in the year 1859, may be
traced back to a very early period. Nyren was
the first who protested against it. He says—
"I conceive, then, that all the fine style of
hitting must in a very material degree cease,
if the modern innovation of throwing instead
of bowling the ball be not discontinued. It
is not the least important objection I have to
offer against the system to say, that it reduces
the strikers too much to an equality, since the
indifferent batsman possesses as fair a chance
of success as the most refined player; and the
reason of this is obvious, because, from the
random manner of delivering the ball, it is
impossible for the fine batsman to have time
for that *finesse* and delicate management which
so peculiary distinguishes the elegant man-
œuvering of the chief players who occupied
the field about eight, ten, or more years ago.
If the system continue, I freely confess that I
cannot even hope again to witness such
exquisite finish as distinguished the playing
of such men as Old Small, and Aylward, the
two Walkers, Beldham, and Lord Frederick
Beauclerc: the last indeed, I believe it is pretty

well understood, retired as soon as the present system was tolerated. I am aware that the defence which has been urged in behalf of throwing is, ' that it tends to shorten the game' —that now a match is commonly decided in one day, which heretofore occupied three times the space in completion. This argument, I grant, is not an irrational one; but if the object in countenancing the innovation (and one be it observed in direct defiance of a standing law) extend solely to the curtailment of the game, why not multiply the difficulties in another direction? Why not give more room for the display of skill in the batter? Why not have four stumps instead of three, and increase the length of the bails from eight inches to ten?"

From the extract given it will be seen that Nyren made a strong opposition to round-arm bowling when it was first introduced.

Straight-arm delivery followed the round-arm system, and with immense success to the Kent Club. This latter system required a peculiar knack, which, Nyren says, was never so faithfully performed as by the member of the Kent Club who introduced it.

For round-arm and swift bowling those who

stand behind and about the batsman's wicket generally wear leg and shin paddings: these are now made with great care; and after the studied consideration of experienced cricketers. It is impossible to do without these cumbersome protectors when standing at the wicket for the purpose of stopping strong round-arm balls. The knee-pan also is always in danger from bowling, unless protected by a padding.

It is impossible at all times to avoid bruises, I therefore recommend all cricketers to be provided for them with a remedy. Felix strongly recommends the use of a little sweet oil, as the "sovereign'st thing on earth for an outward bruise."

HINTS TO YOUNG BOWLERS.

HOLD the ball rather askew; and let the tips of the fingers touch the seam: this will make the ball twirl—a very desirable feature in bowling. Do not hold the ball in the palm of the hand, but in the fingers.

Accustom yourself to a *short* run on delivering the ball, and so save yourself unnecessary fatigue.

A man short in stature and not over strong, cannot bowl fast : he had better confine himself entirely to slow bowling, without attempting that which he can never perform well.

Endeavour to deliver the ball so that it twirls well. Bowl with decision as well as precision. Keep your full face and shoulders square to the opposite wicket. The length at which you pitch the ball, should always depend on the style of play of the batsman opposed to you : more particularly with reference to the forward style of play, and the backward style. But see further as to this, under the head, " FINISHING LESSONS."

The error of young bowlers generally, is, that they do not pitch the ball far enough.

It is good bowling to pitch close to the bat ; so as to compel back play and prevent the easier mode, termed " forward play."

Accustom yourself to bowl from both sides of the wickets : sometimes a sudden change of position by the bowler is very trying to the batsman opposed to you. Besides, too, the ground is often better on one side than the other.

The late William Lillywhite's advice was— "In cricket do nothing rashly; therefore, although you should begin bowling resolutely, do not begin at the top of your speed and strength. If you begin like a lion, you will soon end like a lamb."

THE BOWLER.

" Ye bowlers, take heed, to my precepts attend;
  On you the whole fate of the game must depend:
  Spare your vigour at first, now exert all your strength,
  But measure each step, and be sure pitch a length."

CORTON.

THE bowler's duties are arduous; though frequently the key to success or failure in a cricket match.

. The principal objects to attain in good bowling are few, but important: they comprise straightness and accuracy, with a high delivery: and of these, the latter is perhaps the greatest acquisition in bowling.

Nyren says—" The three best qualities in this important person in the game, are, a high delivery, an upright body, and for his balls to be pitched a proper length. Without these requisites no man can be an effective bowler."

There are many other hints which may be given to a young bowler, in addition to those already stated at page 33. In the first place he should always bowl *within* his strength, not to the utmost of it.

He should not be too systematic in delivery; but occasionally varying his style, pace, and pitch: particularly when bowling to a troublesome batter. Young. bowlers, in their training, should be cautious never to exhaust their strength: as soon as fatigue is felt, they should resign their post to another person.

A bad bowler may soon lose his party the game: and it should be remembered, that whilst such an one pleases his opponents, he vexes and disheartens his own party.

When bowling to a troublesome player, it is sometimes good policy to pitch a ball a little wide of the off stump; because such may lead the striker into giving a chance of a catch.

But the bowler had always best use his discretion with a troublesome player: he may often succeed in putting him out by a sudden change in the rate or pitch of his balls.

When there are two sticklers at the wickets, it is sometimes advisable to change the bowler; and the greater the difference in their styles of bowling the better.

For *swift bowling*, he should pitch the balls about five yards in front of the wicket, so that it bounds straight among the stumps.

For *moderately swift bowling*, he will find the most accurate pitch to be, about four yards in front of the wicket.

And for *slow bowling*, the pitch should be a yard or more nearer the wicket.

It is a very good plan to select an object at a measured distance as your bowling aim; and always pitch the ball at it.

Having once acquired a steady uniformity in the pace of your bowling; and ascertained the exact length at which to pitch the ball with truest effect; the more strictly you adhere to the same pace and pitch, the more successful will be your bowling.

A mark on the ground is often objected to: but a slight difference in the colour of the grass, or any worn place or other visible mark, will suffice to a good eye: and enable him to measure his lengths accordingly.

The bowler often has to do a little fielding at the wicket, such as stopping balls to prevent runs, catching out the striker, &c. In fact it is his duty to be wicket-keeper at his own wicket.

A slow bowler never bowls well with the wind in his face. In a strong breeze the wickets should be pitched across wind.

When the bowler has the choice, he should look out that he has not to bowl in the face of the sun.

The late William Lillywhite, among his hints to bowlers, gives the following excellent advice:—

" Bear in mind the game is never won *till it's lost*, and that is not till the *last* wicket is floored or the runs obtained; and from the glorious uncertainty of it, never give a chance away by the often mistaken notion of the ease with which you can win it. First win it, then enjoy your victory."

THE WICKET-KEEPER.

" The wickets are pitched now, and measured the ground;
Then they form a large ring and stand gazing around:
Since Ajax fought Hector, in sight of all Troy,
No contest was seen with such fear and such joy."
COTTON.

THE wicket-keeper's is the least enviable position, during hard bowling, of any in the field; though it is at all times a most important one. His proper place is at the striker's wicket; or

at a very short distance behind it : consequently,
he is exposed to the fury and swiftness of all
the balls which the striker fails to stop. It is
his duty to endeavour, to the utmost of his skill,
to catch or stop the ball in the event of the
batsman failing to do so: he is therefore, of
necessity, liable to many hard knocks and
bruises; particularly from swift bowling. Of
late years it has been usual for the wicket-keeper
to use a padding for the legs and other parts of
the body, when exposed to the terrific fire of a
strong round-arm bowler ; or his position would
be one of danger.

The movements of all the fieldsmen are under
the supervision of the wicket-keeper : he must
know the position in the field that each man
should occupy; and direct them accordingly.
He "shifts" the fieldsmen from time to time,
by merely motioning with his hand; and it is
their duty to obey. They should be placed in
such a manner that all may have their eyes on
the batsman, as well as the wicket-keeper.

The moment the bowler is ready, the wicket-
keeper takes his stand behind the wicket, and
he has no business to move, so as to interrupt
either the bowler or the striker. He should

stand in a stooping position, with legs apart, the left foot being in advance ; and the hands ready to catch the ball, the left hand being uppermost: and he must stand close enough to reach the wicket.

He must do his best to stump out the batsman. But he should never attempt to put the wicket down, unless there is a chance of putting out the striker.

He should, as much as possible, avoid knocking the wicket down.

He must watch the bowler very closely, and keep his eye on the ball from the moment of its leaving the bowler's hands.

The wicket-keeper may, if he thinks proper, shift the fieldsmen unknown to the batter. And he will often find it necessary to draw them in closer, or send them farther off, according to the different changes in the bowling, or the known skill of the batter.

It is necessary in arranging the field, that the wicket-keeper should take into consideration the powers and general play of the batsmen, and place the fieldsmen accordingly.

When the ball is thrown from the field to the wicket-keeper, he should stand close to, and

with his hands inclining towards the wicket, in
order that a second of time be not lost, but
rather that the ball may be instantly dropped
upon the wicket.

On the wicket-keeper putting down a wicket,
he should wait until the umpire has said " out !"
before he tosses up the ball as a signal of victory
to the fieldsmen and others.

THE UMPIRE.

THE umpire's is an important but onerous
office. He should not only be well experienced
in the game, but he must also be a man of the
strictest honour and integrity; and very attentive to his duties.

His duty, in the first place, is to pitch the
wickets, attend to the preliminary arrange-
ments, and call the players to their posts.

He has to settle, at once, on being appealed
to, all disputes and doubts connected with the
play: and there is no appeal from his decision.

Two umpires are required in a cricket-match.
One is placed at the bowler's wicket, in a line
directly behind it: in which position he is
enabled to see whether the ball goes in a straight

line to the opposite wicket: and in the event of
the ball being stopped by the striker's leg, he
must decide at once whether or no, if it had not
been so stopped, it would have hit the wicket:
and if so he must give him out as—" leg before
wicket !" It is his duty to watch the bowler
and players, and see that no infringement of the
rules is attempted.

The other umpire is placed at the striker's
wicket; partly behind it, but so as not to interrupt the movements of the fieldsmen, or the
wicket-keeper. Yet so that he can command a
full view of the batsman and his position; and
be able to give his decision clearly and promptly
when attempts are made to put him out.

THE SCORERS.

Two scorers are required in a cricket-match;
viz. one for each side. Their position should be
such as to command a full view of the play,
without being in the way of the fieldsmen.

Their duty is to watch the game with close
observation. A scorer should not be dependent
on others or on his co-scorer for results; but
rely entirely on himself.

He should never allow bystanders to intrude upon him: nor should he be interrupted by any one whilst the game is being played.

A fully filled, truthful, and carefully noted score-sheet is the best and most perfect epitome of the game.

SCORING-SHEETS.

PRINTED scoring-sheets may now be had of all venders of cricketing accoutrements. A supply should always be kept in hand by the secretary to every cricket-club. A form of a scoring-sheet is given on the next page: there should be as many lines ruled as there are players: and the form, with the same headings (excepting the two first colums) being extended, and copied and printed on a sheet of foolscap paper, it will then be complete for first and second innings.

E

FORM OF SCORING-SHEET.

Match Played at   *on*   186

Order of Going in.	Name of Batsman.	How out.	Name of Bowler.	Number of Runs Obtained.	Total.
1					
2					
3					
4					
5					
6					
7					
8					
9					
10					
11					
	Wide balls				
	No balls				
	Byes				
	Leg-byes				

THE BATSMAN OR STRIKER.

"Ye strikers observe when the foe shall draw nigh—
Mark the bowler, advancing with vigilant eye ;
Your skill all depends upon distance and sight,
Stand firm to your scratch, let your bat be upright."

COTTON.

THIS player is always the chief object of
attraction in the game: not only to all the
fieldsmen and others concerned in the play,
but especially so to bystanders, betting-persons,
and others interested in the results of the game.
He is indeed "the observed of all observers."
He has to contend against the efforts of the
fieldsman, the wicket-keeper, and the bowler,
all of whom do their best to put him out: the
bowler in particular, tries by every legitimate
means in his power to puzzle and put out the
batsman; who has to defend his wicket by skill
and with the use of the bat, and so endeavour
to prevent the whole field (eleven in number)
from putting him out whilst the ball is "in
play." When the ball is not actually in play it
is considered "dead;" and when dead it cannot
be used for putting out the striker.

The batsman should never forget that his skill depends mainly on the unison of action between the eye and the hand: and in this respect batting resembles shooting. The author of a very able little treatise on shooting, called " The Dead Shot," says—" the hand and the eye must act both at once, as if connected by electricity:" a remark which applies with equal and unabated force to good batting : for if the eye fails to obey the hand or the hand the eye, at the very instant of striking the ball, there can be no certainty as to the result : in fact you probably miss the ball altogether.

On taking his stand at the wicket the batsman should place the bat upright from the ground in front of the popping-crease. He should always accustom himself to the proper positions : there must be no negligence or carelessness in his demeanour at the wicket : he should stand easy, and in the best position for hitting: the legs not too wide apart, or in striking he will be very likely to miss the ball by hitting *under* it.

Nyren's golden rules to young batsmen are simply these—

" The body and bat upright—the hands near to each other— the left elbow well turned up— and the legs not too much extended."

Just before the ball is delivered, raise the bat steadily, so as to be prepared for any emergency; and when you see whereabouts the ball will pitch, you must use your discretion as to what you will do.

And the batsman should remember that he cannot hit well or effectively if his arm or wrist be held in a stiff or awkward manner : both arm and wrist must be allowed full play and elasticity. Pycroft says, in the " Cricket-Field," of a clumsy batsman—"His elbow seems glued to his side, his shoulder stiff at the joint ; and the little speed of his bat depends on a twist and a wriggle of his whole body."

The batsman should bear in mind that it is highly advantageous to play at points which enable him to direct the ball clear of the fieldsmen.

The batsman must never dispute with the umpire ; but rather bow to his decision without a murmur.

THE FIELDSMEN.

" Ye fieldsmen look sharp, lest your pains ye beguile ;
   Move close like an army, in rank and in file ;
   When the ball is returned, back it sure, for I trow,
   Whole states have been ruined by one overthrow."

COTTON.

THE fieldsmen are those persons who are
arranged about the field at certain distances
from the wickets : their duty is to watch the
ball, and return it to the wicket-keeper with all
possible expedition ; the object being to endeavour to prevent their opponents, the batsmen at
the wickets, from getting runs. The fieldsmen
are recognized by the name of the position
allotted to them in the field ; viz.: Point, Cover-
point, Mid-wicket, Short-slip, Long-slip, Long-
stop, Long-field off, Long-field on, Long-leg, &c.

The duties assigned to each of these in the
field, will be separately discussed in the following pages. They are generally arranged according to their individual efficiency. All fieldsmen should be stationed so as to have a good
view of the batsman. They should always be

on the *qui vive*, and endeavour to "get the start of the ball."

They should never get in the way of each other, nor in front of the wicket-keeper, so as to intercept the ball thrown to him from the field. But they should always back up willingly: by neglecting to do so, many a match is lost.

In backing up, always take care to keep at least twelve yards apart from the fieldsman in front of you.

Fieldsmen should be cautious never to return the ball violently or carelessly, but always with accuracy, expedition, and discretion. On throwing the ball home, always let the top of the stumps be your mark.

Whenever any one of the fieldsmen (no matter what his position) finds the ball coming towards him swiftly and low, or bounding; in order to make sure of stopping it he should go down on one knee; by which means (with practice) he will make certain of stopping it; for if he misses it with his hands, his body will form a butt, and the progress of a swift or bounding ball may be so stopped with certainty.

The arrangment of the fieldsmen rests, as before stated, with the wicket-keeper, and it is the duty of every fieldsman to obey his directions and take the position allotted to him. The wicket-keeper, however, must remember that slow bowling requires a very different arrangement to that of fast bowling. For slow, the fieldsmen are stationed nearer the wickets; and for fast, they are placed much farther off.

LONG-STOP.

THE place for this fieldsman is behind the wicket-keeper.

His duty is to stop the ball when the batsman and wicket-keeper both fail to do so. He should stand in, so as to save the one run. In every instance when the ball comes into his hands he should instantly return it to the wicket-keeper.

He has also to cover many of the slips from the bat, which come nearer to him than to other fieldsmen; and whether to the leg or off side.

A judicious and active *long-stop* may generally prevent his adversary from getting many runs: and he may often surprise the batsman by rapidly returning the ball.

Against rapid bowling he should go down on his right knee, hold his hands ready to catch;

and then if he misses the ball with his hands, it will be stopped by his body.

POINT.

THE position of this fieldsman is sometimes dangerous, unless he is very quick and active in his movements.

He stands directly opposite the popping-crease, at a distance of only four yards, or from that to seven, from the point of the striker's bat. During slow or steady bowling he stands at the near distance: for rapid bowling the farther, and a little behind the popping-crease.

It is the duty of this fieldsman to watch, minutely, the batsman's actions: and be always ready and guarded.

At the moment of the ball being bowled, he should stand with his legs a little apart; his hands open, and prepared to catch the ball, though it comes swiftly or suddenly towards him.

When the batsman is about to block the ball, the man at point should move in closer.

Point is always considered a distinguished position in great matches.

SHORT-SLIP.

THE place for this fieldsman is, between the wicket-keeper and point: but a little farther from the latter than from the former. He should be very active in his limbs, and must have a sharp quick eye.

He should stand with his legs apart, and hands ready, from the moment of the ball leaving the bowler's hands ; for it sometimes flies towards him like a cannon-shot ; and with all the suddenness imaginable.

He should back up behind the wicket-keeper when the ball is thrown in : and whenever the wicket-keeper has to leave his post for a ball, it is *short-slip's* duty to step up and occupy it until his return.

LONG-SLIP.

THIS is a trying position during fast bowling. Long-slip must be an active and good fieldsman : his position is at an angle with short-slip and point, and usually at about the same distance from the wicket as long-stop. He is placed so as to cover short-slip and prevent the one run.

COVER-POINT.

THIS is a very important fieldsman in a cricket-match. It has been said, with much truth, that to perform his duty well, *cover-point* should be a good tactician. He should not be pinned to any precise position.

It is his duty to watch narrowly the movements and actions of the batsman. And he will often find it his duty to advance to meet the ball, and cover mid-wicket and point.

He should be able to judge as to which direction the ball will take, the moment he sees the action of the batsman: and so he will often be enabled to get the start of the ball.

This fieldsman will frequently have catches come in his way; and sometimes difficult ones.

MID-WICKET.

THE position this fieldsman occupies is, on the off side, half way between cover-point and the bowler.

He should be lively and quick; for he will sometimes have plenty of work: and he must be able to throw with precision; so as to return the ball promptly into the wicket-keeper's hands.

Many chances of catching occur to this fieldsman; and lots of close struggles offer for putting out the batsman. He has constant work: therefore activity and watchfulness are the most essential qualifications.

He takes the bowler's place *pro tem.* when the bowler is obliged to leave for the purpose of stopping the ball.

LONG-FIELD OFF.

By "off" is meant the off side of the wicket. The position of this fieldsman is in the discretion of the wicket-keeper, and is generally regulated more or less according to the batting and bowling; but he is always placed on the off side between the bowler and mid-wicket: and out far enough in the field to save the two runs.

His duty is to cover the positions of mid-wicket and bowler. He should be active in his limbs and able to throw well and run fast.

LONG-FIELD ON.

THIS fieldsman stands on the opposite side of the wicket to that of the *long-field off.*

When the bowling is steady, and the hitting not severe, he may be brought in to save the one run: but it is usual for him to stand out some distance from the bowler, so as to save the two runs.

This fieldsman also should be a good runner and accurate thrower.

LONG-FIELD TO THE HIP.

THE place for this fieldsman is opposite the popping-crease; but standing out so as to save two runs. He is sometimes moved in to save the one run: but this only when the batting is feeble, or the bowling slow and steady.

He should be able to throw and run well, and always endeavour to get the start of the ball by running soon enough.

LONG-LEG.

IT is indispensably necessary that this fieldsman should have superior strength of arm, and be able to throw well.

His position is far out in the field, in the direction in which the ball generally goes when hit very hard, and under favourable circumstances, by the batsman.

His duty is to prevent his adversaries from making four runs at a single stroke from the bat.

This fieldsman must be attentive in backing up behind those fieldsmen which may be nearest him.

FINISHING LESSONS.

ON THE USE OF THE CRICKET-BAT.

HAVING long practised and become well grounded in the rudimentary lessons, the young cricketer should attentively consider the more advanced and scientific practice; so as to acquire a graceful, or polished, as well as a safe, certain, and highly effective mode of using the bat.

The great beauty of batting is, that of sending the ball skimming along just above the ground: such are the hits by which the greatest number of runs are obtained; and no chance is given to the fieldsmen of catching out the striker.

It is not good play to strike at, or block those balls which come five or six inches or more higher than the bails: it is always best to let them pass; indeed, it is dangerous to strike at them, because of the great risk of being caught out. Therefore, unless the striker is well skilled in the art of *hitting the ball down*, he had better play the safer game of allowing it to pass by.

At *ground-balls* the batsman must play with caution. A ground-ball is that which bounds and leaps along, or rather, strikes the ground more than once in its course from the bowler's hands to the batsman's wicket. These are always deceptive and uncertain balls to play at: and of all others, the most likely, when bowled a little wide, to take a turn and go smash! into the wicket. The batsman had better guard his wicket with double vigilance against a ground-ball.

A *shooting-ball* is that which, instead of rising from the spot where it is pitched, shoots along the ground, or just above it. Unless a shooting-ball is played at or blocked with great promptitude and precision, it will shoot into the wicket. It is a very destructive ball, and troublesome to most players.

Play at shooting-balls with extra quickness, or they will assuredly deceive you. Never strike at them when they are going straight for the wicket. Stop them by playing the bat back; and as near to the wicket as is consistent with safety from touching it.

Length balls, are those which are pitched on the ground in front of the wicket at such a well measured or puzzling length that, unless blocked or struck as they rise, they bound into the wicket. And such is the old and most admired style of bowling. The striker must be well guarded and prepared for length balls, or he will assuredly learn, on allowing them to pass, that they have found their way to his stumps.

Whenever you can conveniently reach and cover a length ball at the pitch, do so by playing forward.

The cut is one of the most brilliant hits in the game. It is better adapted to underhand bowling: and since the round-arm style has been introduced, the cut is not very often attempted.

There can be no cut unless the ball rises: and the cutter must begin in time to lift his bat above his shoulder; and be careful to cut slantwise, so that the ball does not fly up in the air.

In the cut the batsman uses his bat somewhat horizontally; he must not lose sight of the ball as it rises from the ground: the very fact of good sight at the ball at the moment of striking

F

is the secret of an effective cut: and the cut applies to short pitched balls; not long hops.

Mr. Bradshaw, a celebrated cricketer of the Midland Counties, formerly famed for his splendid cuts, gives the following definition as to the best mode of cutting:—the batsman should " cut from the bails between short-slip and point, with a late horizontal bat—cutting never by guess, but always by sight, at the ball itself; the cut applying to rather short pitched balls, not actually long hops ; and that not being properly a cut which is in advance of the point."

The *forward cut*, also called the *forward lounge*, is an off hit. It is generally made at balls which are too wide and near the ground for the backward cut. The result of the forward cut when well made is, that the batsman sends the ball between point and mid-wicket.

The *half volley*.—This is an important stroke in batting, it occurs when the batter hits the ball just as it rises from the pitch, taking it in that part of the bat where the force tells with greatest effect.

The three chief points to observe in this hit

are, first, to time the ball with precision: second, to hit it at the very nick of time, as it rises from the ground : and third, to be careful not to give a chance of a catch to the fieldsmen.

The *tice* is a ball that is dropped as it were at nearly the full pitch. This is a difficult and uncertain ball ; and one from which it is seldom that more than one run can be obtained ; or two at the most ; and frequently none : for it is safer to block it. If you strike you are very apt to miss, because the ball is dropping at the very time at which you strike.

Those balls which, among well practised cricketers, are considered safe or certain strokes, are all loose balls, or badly bowled balls : that is to say, if left untouched by the batsman, the probability is they would not hit the wicket ; or at all events they offer so fair a chance to the striker that he may safely venture on striking them boldly.

It is not *all* badly-bowled balls, however, that are "certain hits :" indeed the fairest offers from the bowler's hands sometimes deceive the most experienced players : and in this respect cricketing may be compared with shooting.

Like the fairest chances at birds on wing, the most skilful sportsmen sometimes fail to bring them down. So with the cricketer, if ever so skilled, he occasionally misses his mark, and finds the ball among his stumps. High dropping balls are called "tosses" and "tices;" that is, pitched high, so as to drop into the wicket without grounding: a toss or a tice is always an awkward ball, and often puts out the best player, when all other styles of bowling fail.

Leaping balls are those which rise from the spot at which pitched, as high or higher than the bails.

The batsman should be careful, and play at these behind the popping-crease; and stop them by lifting the bat from the ground; holding it in the position already indicated at page 65 for stopping *length balls ;* and taking especial care that the *left elbow is raised.* In this manner a leaping ball may be effectually stopped, and no chance of a catch will be given.

When a leaping ball seems to be going higher than the bails, either remove your bat out of the way and let the ball pass, or strike it down.

The man at *point* is the foe to the batsman who attempts to stop a leaping ball. If *point*

gets in close (which he will do if up to his
work), though the batsman stops the ball ever
so cleverly, point will be very likely to catch
him out. It is therefore better to let the ball
pass when going higher than the bail, unless
you have time for a slashing hit.

The *off hit* may be made at the ball with
boldness and safety when pitched anywhere on
the off side within two feet of the wicket, but
beyond that distance the batsman had better
leave it alone. The off hit is performed with
the bat held upright.

When the ball is pitched rather short of a
length on the off side of the wicket, it is sometimes played at with the bat held upright or
perpendicularly; and sometimes horizontally.
Among the best of cricketers, it will be found
that some play at it in one way and some in the
other. When about to play at a ball of the sort,
the batsman should move his left foot forward
across the wicket; by which means he will
acquire greater power over the ball.

Nyren always considered it safer to play at
these balls with the bat held perpendicularly:
though, unquestionably, the bolder and more
brilliant mode of play was horizontally.

Leg hits. There are three of these: the draw, forward leg hit, and the backward leg hit.

When the ball is pitched *inside the near (or leg stump)*, step back with the right foot ; play as near the wicket as convenient, and with the bat upright. This is one of the safest balls at which you can play : and when hit hard, many runs may be made off it. Let the ball go nearly into the leg stump, and then glance it off. Always make it a rule to play boldly at balls pitched on the near side of the wicket; hit them hard and rather on the top, so as to drive them along the ground on the near side.

When the ball is pitched *wide of the wicket on the near side*, and you wish to make the *forward leg hit*, move very quickly in front of the wicket, turn half round, and strike the ball hard, driving it behind the wicket. A good hit of this kind is almost always certain for three or four runs, and sometimes more; particularly with a rapid bowler ; because the batter accelerates the speed of the ball by driving it in the same direction as that in which it was going ; and to a part of the field where there is, probably, no one to stop it.

Young batsmen are seldom quick enough for

these hits ; and therein lies the whole secret of
this mode of play at leg balls.

Skilful and old-practised cricketers, sometimes,
instead of striking at a leg-ball, perform what is
termed *the draw :*—that is, hold the bat in the
same position as if for a home-block, and then
just recede the body to get clear of the ball, and
turn the face of the bat a little round towards
your legs, just so that the ball may graze the bat
and glance off, which it often does at a terrific
pace, giving the batsman an opportunity of
adding three or four to his score.

Another mode of performing the draw is,
when the ball comes in straight for the top of
the leg stump : in which case you suspend the
bat from the wrists, and draw the ball to the leg.
The draw, however, should not be attempted by
inexperienced hands ; and never except to swift
bowling : the best mode of acquiring the art is,
by long and frequent practice to slow bowling :
and so gradually increasing the pace.

Bear in mind this important distinction ;—
when the ball is pitched *beyond a length on the
near side*, it should be *blocked :* the bat must
be held in the same position as for stopping a
length ball ; viz., with the left elbow raised.

In this case do not strike too soon, or you will drive the ball into the bowler's hands.

The secret or difficulty in making the off cut, leg hit, and other distinguished strokes of the bat, lies in the art of timing the ball exactly, as to its pitch, bound, and distance wide of the wicket. These hits are one and all often missed in swift bowling by the best players.

All hits may be more or less well made according to the calculation, by the striker, of time, pitch, and bound, from the moment the ball leaves the bowler's hands.

In all hitting be careful to turn the blade of the bat a little over the ball.

STRAY HINTS.

In your practice, always play as if in a match. Attend to your running: let your motto be "ever ready; ever nimble."

When at the wicket, if a struck ball goes behind you, do not turn round to look after it, but attend to and rely on your companion at the opposite wicket, as to the expediency or safety of a run: and after one run, and when you have changed places and the ball is still in the field, he will depend on you as to the expediency of a second run.

Always run when a catch is given; because you can but be caught out; and if the fieldsman misses the ball, you are safe to have made your run before he can pick up the ball and return it to the wicket keeper.

Tight bracing, like tight lacing, is injurious to the health and opposed to the free use of the limbs. The cricketer requires the greatest possible freedom from all straps and bandages, which impede the use of the legs and arms.

Never make hazardous runs: it is better to lose a run than to run a risk of losing a wicket.

Never attempt hazardous batting, and so incur the risk of losing your place at the wicket: random batting never succeeds against good bowling, and seldom against bad.

Random bowling, like reckless striking, never succeeds.

In the game of cricket a great deal depends on chance: an unlucky ball may put out the best player.

All cricketers, from the batsman downwards, should be careful when in the cricket-field never to lose either their temper or their confidence.

The Original Laws of Cricket,

REVISED AND CORRECTED UP TO THE YEAR 1861.

THE CRICKET-BALL

1. Should not weigh less than five ounces and a half, nor more than five ounces and three quarters. It should measure not less than nine inches, nor more than nine inches and one quarter in circumference. At the beginning of each innings, either party to be at liberty to call for a new ball.

THE CRICKET-BAT

2. Should not exceed four inches and one quarter in width at the widest part; nor more than thirty-eight inches in length, handle included.

THE STUMPS

3. Should be three in number; each standing twenty-seven inches in height above ground; the bails being eight inches in length; the stumps to be of equal and sufficient thickness to prevent the ball passing between them.

THE BOWLING-CREASE

4. Should be in a line with the stumps; six feet
eight inches in length, the stumps in the
centre, with a return crease at each end
towards the bowler at right angles.

THE POPPING-CREASE

5. Should be four feet from the wicket, and parallel
with it; no limit as to length, but not
shorter than the bowling-crease.

THE WICKETS

6. Should be pitched directly opposite to each other
by the umpires; the space of twenty-two
yards intervening between the wickets.

7 It is not lawful for either party during a match,
without the consent of the other, to roll,
water, cover, mow, or beat the ground, except
at the commencement of each innings, when
the ground may be swept and rolled at the
request of either party; such request to be
made to one of the umpires within two
minutes after the conclusion of the former
innings. This rule is not intended to
prevent the striker from beating the ground
with his bat about the spot at which he

stands during the innings, nor to prevent the bowler from filling up holes in any manner he may think proper, when the ground is wet.

8. After rain the wickets may be changed with the consent of both parties.

THE BOWLER

9. To deliver the ball with one foot on the ground behind the bowling-crease, and within the return-crease, and to bowl four balls before changing wickets, which he shall be permitted to do once only during the same innings.

10. The ball must be bowled. If thrown or jerked, or if the bowler raise his hand or arm above his shoulder, in delivering the ball, the umpire shall call "No Ball."

11. The bowler may require the striker at the wicket from which he is bowling to stand on either side of the wicket as he may direct.

12. If the bowler toss the ball over the striker's head, or bowl it so wide that in the opinion of the umpire it was not fairly within reach of the batsman, he shall adjudge one run to the parties, either with or without an appeal; the run to be put down to the score

of wide balls: and such balls shall not be reckoned as one of the four balls referred to in Rule 9; but if the batsman by any means, bring himself within reach of the ball, the run shall not be scored.

13. If the bowler deliver a "No Ball," or a "Wide Ball," the striker to be allowed as many runs as he can get, and he shall not be out, except by running out: and in the event of no run being obtained, then one shall be added to the score of "No Balls," or "Wide Balls," as the case may be. The names of the bowlers who bowl "Wide Balls," or "No Balls," to be put down on the scoring-sheet.

14. At the beginning of each innings, the umpire to call "Play;" from which time to the end of the innings, no trial ball shall be allowed.

THE STRIKER TO BE OUT

15. If either of the bails are bowled off, or if a stump is bowled out of the ground.

16. Or, if the ball from the stroke of the bat or hand, but not the wrist, be caught or held before it touch the ground, although it be hugged to the body of the catcher.

17. Or, if on or after striking, or at any other time while the ball is in play, both his feet are out-

side the popping-crease, and his wicket put
down (except his bat be grounded within it).

18. Or, if in striking at the ball, he hit down his
wicket, or knock off either of the bails.

19. Or, if under pretence of running, or otherwise,
either of the strikers prevent a ball from
being caught, the striker of the ball to be the
party out.

20. Or, if the ball is struck or blocked and he wil-
fully strikes it again.

21. Or, if in running, the wicket is struck down
with the ball, by a throw, or by the hand or
arm (with ball in hand) before his bat (in
hand) or some part of his person is grounded
over or within the popping-crease. But if
both bails are off, a stump must be knocked
down.

22. Or, if any part of the striker's dress knock down
the wicket.

23. Or, if the striker touch, or take up the ball
during the play, unless at the request of the
opposite party.

24. Or, if with any part of his person he stop or
impede the ball which, in the opinion of the
umpire at the bowler's wicket, had been
pitched in a straight line with the striker's
wicket, and would have hit it.

MISCELLANEOUS LAWS.

25. In running, if the players have crossed each other, he that runs for the wicket which is put down is out.

26. On a ball being caught, no run to be scored.

27. A striker being run out, the run is incomplete and must not be scored.

28. If "lost ball" is called, the striker to be allowed six runs ; but if more than six have been run before "lost ball" has been called, then all which have been run to be scored.

29. After the ball is finally settled in the wicket—keeper's or bowler's hands, or has passed through the hands of the wicket-keeper for the bowler to resume bowling, it is considered dead ; but when the bowler is about to deliver the ball, if the striker at his wicket go outside the popping-crease, before such actual delivery, the said bowler may put him out, unless his bat (in hand) or some part of his person be grounded over or within the popping-crease.

30. The striker must not retire from his wicket and then return to it for the purpose of completing his innings, after another has been in, without the consent of the opposite party.

LAWS AFFECTING SUBSTITUTES.

81. A substitute must not, in any case, be allowed to stand out or run between the wickets for another player, without the consent of the opposite party; and in case of such consent being given, the striker is out if either he or his substitute be outside the popping-crease whilst the ball is in play, in manner mentioned in Laws 17 and 21.

82. In all cases where a substitute is allowed, the consent of the opposite party must also be obtained as to the person to act as substitute, and the place in the field which he shall take.

FIELDING, &c.

83. If any fieldsman stop the ball with his hat or cap, the ball so stopped must immediately be considered dead, and the opposite party may add five runs to their score; but if any have been run before the ball was so stopped, they shall score no more than five for the run.

84. The ball having been hit, the striker may guard the wicket with his bat, or with any part of his body except his hands, so that the 23rd Law may not be infringed.

G

WICKET-KEEPER.

35. The wicket-keeper must not use the ball for the purpose of stumping until it has passed the wicket; nor may he, by any noise or movement, incommode the striker; and if any part of his person be over or before the wicket, although the ball hit the wicket, the striker is not to be out.

THE UMPIRES.

36. The umpires to be the sole judges of fair and unfair play, and all disputes must be determined by them, each at his own wicket; but in case of the ball being caught, and the umpire at the bowling-wicket being unable to decide with satisfaction to himself, he may apply to the other umpire, whose opinion must be conclusive.

37. The umpires in all matches must pitch the wickets fairly; and the parties must toss for the choice of innings. The umpires should shift their quarters to the opposite wicket after each party has had one innings.

38. They must allow two minutes for each striker to come to the wicket, and ten minutes between

each innings. When the umpires call "Play," the party refusing to play loses the match.

39. The umpires are not to order a striker out unless appealed to by the adversaries.

40. But if one of the bowler's feet be not on the ground behind the bowling-crease, and within the return-crease when he delivers the ball, the umpire at the bowling-wicket, without any appeal, must call "No Ball."

41. If either of the strikers, in running, fail to go the full distance, the umpire must call "One short."

42. Neither of the umpires shall be allowed to bet.

43. Neither of the umpires can be changed during a match, without the consent of both parties, except in case of a violation of the 42nd Law; in which case either party may dismiss the transgressor.

44. After the delivery of four balls, the umpire must call "Over," but not until the ball is finally settled in the wicket-keeper's or bowler's hands: after which, if a suggestion be made to the umpire that either of the strikers is out, a question may be put previously to, but not after, the delivery of the next ball.

45. When necessary to call "No Ball," the umpire

must do so immediately upon delivery: and "Wide Ball," as soon as it has passed the striker.

MATCHES (SECOND INNINGS).

46. The players who go in second, must follow on with their second innings, if they have obtained eighty runs less than their antagonists; except, in all matches limited to one day's play, when the number should be limited to sixty instead of eighty.

CRICKET-MATCHES.

" Here's guarding and catching, and throwing, and
    tossing,
And bowling, and striking, and running, and crossing;
Each mate must excel in some principal part—
The Pentathlum of Greece could not show so much art."

THERE is something truly ennobling in a cricket-
match. It is soul-stirring alike to the players
as to the beholders. The fair sex, too, take
deep interest in the game—as they do in all
innocent recreations—and watch both the play
and players with much concern during the
excitement of a public contest.

" The parties are met and arrayed all in white;
Famed Elis ne'er boasted so pleasing a sight:
Each nymph looks askew at her favourite swain,
And views him half-stript both with pleasure and pain."

With the facilities afforded by railroads for
travelling, cricket-matches are now played in all
parts of the country by the most skilful and
renowned cricketers. The east and the west,
the north and the south counties, each in their
turn, meet and play matches, interchangeably
every year; thus affording young cricketers in

the remotest districts, opportunities of witnessing the finest play and most exquisite *finesse* that .can be seen throughout the land. Such public matches are always attractive, and in some parts are the one great event of the year ; creating as much sensation in the neighbourhood as if they were battles fought with swords and staves.

There is always a manly and generous feeling displayed by all true-hearted cricketers, when victorious, towards those whom they have vanquished. There is, generally speaking, less ill feeling in cricketing contests than in others : and it is well that it should be so, for it frequently happens that the defeated have honourably distinguished themselves : and though oftentimes, at the hands of the critic, there is not left for them even the solace of sympathy, the vanquished eleven find their most cordial admirers among their victors.

Whenever a cricket match is being played—whether by peers or peasants, commoners or professionals, schoolboys or collegians, soldiers or sailors—it is always a centre of attraction. Whether in town or out of town, in crowded parks or secluded villages, every one who passes

by, stops loitering within gaze of the per-
formers, and takes more or less interest in the
play.

As an instance of the increasing popularity
and high countenance of the game of cricket, it
may be mentioned, that among the records of
public matches during the last few years, will be
found several highly distinguished ones : for
instance, the Lords and Commons of England
are represented by twenty-two parliamentary
cricketers against eleven of the I Zingari : the
members of the University of Oxford against
Cambridge, and *vice versa ;* the barristers of the
Home Circuit against the Western Circuit ; Midland Circuit against Oxford Circuit, &c. Fifty
years ago, if a member of the English bar had
indulged in manly games with that spirit and
enthusiasm which a large majority of barristers
now indulge, it would have been impossible for
him to have succeeded in his profession, so
narrow and plodding were the notions of professional life in those days; and if a barrister
wrote a book upon any other subject than the
law, it was a certain blast to his prospects at the
bar ; the foolish notion then prevailing that no
man could be a good lawyer, unless he devoted his

whole time to his profession. But such simple, narrow-minded, and erroneous ideas are now completely ridiculed by all educated men. And it is daily apparent that he who excels in manly games, sports, and recreations such as require skill, science, or precision of the eye and the hand, is the man of all others who eventually excels in his profession.

Instances of the kind are constantly before us at the present day ; and a clearer fact was never established. It seems reasonable enough that the man who, by superior skill, energy, or perseverance, is enabled to surpass his fellows in such recreations as cricket and shooting, with many other sports and games, that man, of all others, is most likely to surpass them in professional, engineering, or other avocations requiring talent and skill ; one is a true test of the other. If a man excels in nothing manly or recreative, without great good luck, he will never excel in any profession.

There needs not a word of proof here, when speaking of that which is familiar to all, viz. that the most distinguished characters in public life, the greatest statesmen, the greatest lawyers, and the most eminent men in the land, have, at some time or other, generally in early life, been *stars* in the field, with the gun or the cricket-bat.

The famous game of cricket is very popular in every University and public school in the kingdom: as our most distinguished public characters come from these; and from the same sources come our most brilliant cricketers.

In conclusion, who can forget the memorable match between England and America, when, in response to a challenge sent us from America, *eleven* cricketers taken from the lists of English professionals crossed the Atlantic, for the very purpose of accepting the challenge, and playing several matches against twenty-two of the best cricketers America could produce. The results were, that in every one of those matches, though a field of twenty-two were opposed to them on each occasion, the English eleven were eminently victorious. A photograph of this memorable trans-Atlantic cricket-match has been taken, in the shape of a group of full-length portraits of the eleven English champion cricketers.

With respect to the general character of cricket-matches by eleven against twenty-two in the field, and which are now of such frequent occurrence, Felix says, "only those who have had to play against these multitudes can tell what it is to get an ordinary average."

It has been said, that at the present day, no nation under the sun can vie with England in the game of cricket,—a remark which needs no confirmation here.

THE CATAPULTA.

THE catapulta was formerly an engine of war, used by the Romans for casting javelins and stones against castellated walls.

A modern form of catapulta has been constructed, with a view to do away with the necessity of bowling the ball.

Professional cricketers, and bowlers in particular, object to it as an innovation: it is however a very useful machine for young cricketers. It may be controlled so as to throw the ball at various paces, and either swiftly or slowly.

Felix, who has written a very amusing and instructive book on cricket, is a great advocate of the catapulta ; he improved on it considerably. Though an old-fashioned machine, the modern form, as now used for cricketing purposes, originated with Felix. To quote his own words, he says :—

" In its original form the history of this machine is traced back to the time of the Romans: when, with its gigantic energies, it could propel to a much greater distance than could the human arm, weighty javelins, large beams of wood headed with iron, and heavy stones."

* * * * . * * *

" In the old-fashioned catapulta the ball was placed in a hollow near the top of the tongue, and the tongue flew up, throwing the ball by the concussion of the tongue, against a piece of oxhide stuffed with leather, making a great noise, and projecting the ball very imperfectly. The next suggestion was, that the ball should be made to rest upon a stage, and struck from it after the manner of a billiard ball. From this moment all began to work well, first leather, as at the end of a cue ; then (as it is now) india-rubber."

The modern catapulta has undergone many improvements: one in particular, of which Felix speaks, viz.—

"A cushion placed upon two iron springs, to receive the tongue immediately after the hammer has struck the ball, thereby relieving the instrument from an immense jarring. The second improvement is, a plate, upon which the ball rests, moving upon a screw laterally, giving a leg or an off ball; and a screw fixed in front immediately under the plate, to alter the angle of projection, causing the ball to pitch at the eighteenth yard, more or less, at pleasure."

*   *   *   *   *

" With the use of this instrument you may (by setting it to the pace, so fast, that it would split your bat in two ; or so slow, that the ball would scarcely reach the wicket) imitate the pace and place of all the great bowlers of the day.

Too much practice, with perfectly and straight bowling would, perhaps, cramp your hitting. The person working it should (unless otherwise required) occasionally vary the direction of the ball, and this (without the knowledge of the batsman) can be done easily in the improved catapulta." *

* Felix " On the Bat."

The catapulta will be found a very useful machine for cricket practice, particularly in the neighbourhood in which good bowlers are scarce ; but it is always objected to in a match.

SINGLE WICKET.

THE number of players, in this game, varies from one to six on a side.

The distance between the bowler's stumps and the batsman's wicket should be twenty-two yards.

The bowler's wicket consists of two stumps, with a bail across the top.

In order to score a run at single wicket, the batsman must go to the bowler's wicket, knock off the bail, and return to the popping-crease at his own wicket.

If the bail happens to be off when the striker arrives at the bowler's wicket, he must knock down a stump.

The striker cannot run when the ball is dead, or in the hands of the bowler : nor after it has crossed the play.

When there are only four players on each side, or less than that number, it is the custom of the game to mark bounds in a straight line on each side of the wicket, extending twenty-two yards from, and parallel with the wicket.

The batsman must always strike the ball on the inside of the bounds, and never behind them. And when the ball is in the field, it must either be thrown back so that it crosses the play between the batsman's wicket and that of the bowler, or it must cross between the bounds and the batsman's wicket, before it can be considered dead.

In putting the batsman out, the wicket must be put down from the front or inside : when the ball has been behind the wicket it is dead.

When there are more than four persons at play on each side, there are no boundary lines ; and single wicket is then subject to the same rules as double wicket.

Laws affecting Single Wicket.

REVISED AND CORRECTED UP TO THE YEAR 1861.

1. When there are fewer than five players on each side, the bounds must be placed at twenty-two yards; in line with the off and leg stumps.

2. The ball must be hit inside the bounds in order to entitle the striker to a run; to obtain which he must touch the opposite bowling stump, or crease, with his bat or some part of his person, or he must go beyond them; returning to the popping-crease, as at double wicket, according to the 21st Law.

3. When the striker hits the ball, one of his feet must be on the ground behind the popping-crease, otherwise the umpire must call, "No Hit."

4. When there are less than five players on a side, neither byes nor overthrows should be allowed, nor can the striker be caught out behind the wicket, nor stumped out.

5. The fieldsmen must return the ball so that it crosses the play between the wicket and the bowling stump, or between the bowling stump and the bounds. The striker may run till the ball is so returned.

6. After the striker has made one run, if he starts again, he must touch the bowling stump and

turn before the ball crosses the play, in order to entitle him to score another run.

7. The striker is entitled to three runs for a "lost ball," and the same number for a ball stopped with hat or cap; with reference to which see the 27th and 33rd Laws of double wicket.

8. When there are more than five players on a side, there should be no bounds. All hits, byes, and overthrows must then be allowed.

9. The bowler is subject to the same laws as at Double Wicket.

10. One minute is allowed between each ball.

CRICKETING BETS.

1. No bet upon any match is payable, unless the match be played out or given up.

2. If the runs of one player be betted against those of another, the bet must depend on the first innings.

3. If the bet is made on both innings, and one party beat the other in one innings, the runs of the first innings alone must determine it.

4. But if the other party take a second innings, then the bet must be determined by the total number scored.

NEW SPORTING PERIODICAL.

Published Monthly, Price 1s. 6d.

BAILY'S MONTHLY MAGAZINE

OF SPORTS AND PASTIMES, AND
RACING REGISTER.

RACING.	CRICKETING.
HUNTING.	ANGLING,
SHOOTING.	ARCHERY.
COURSING.	AQUATICS.

The following Portraits have already appeared—

Hon. Admiral Rous	The Marquis of Exeter
The Duke of Bedford	The Earl of Zetland
The Duke of Beaufort	The Earl of Derby
George Payne, Esq.	The Earl of Chester-
The Earl of Glasgow	field.

The Leading Professional Sporting Writers are engaged upon the Work, assisted by Amateurs of known proficiency in their several departments of the Sports of the Field.

LONDON :—BAILY BROTHERS, CORNHILL.

HANDBOOKS OF FIELD-SPORTS, ETC.

In Foolscap Octavo, price 2s. 6d. each.

THE DOG; AND HOW TO BREAK HIM: with His Diseases and Methods of Cure. By J. B. JOHNSON. Second Edition, Revised and Enlarged.

THE GUN; AND HOW TO USE IT: By J. B. JOHNSON. Second Edition, Revised and Enlarged.

THE HORSE; AND HOW TO RIDE HIM; A Treatise on the Art of Riding and Leaping. Containing also Explanations as to Ages and Qualities of Horses, Colt-breaking &c. &c. With Practical Lessons on the Management and Control of Saddle Horses; intended for young Equestrians of both sexes., By JOHN BUTLER.

THE FISHING-ROD; AND HOW TO USE IT; A Treatise on the Various Arts of Angling, Trolling, and Fly-fishing. By GLENFIN.

THE CRICKET-BAT; AND HOW TO USE IT; A Treatise on the Game of Cricket; with Practical and Scientific Instructions in Batting, Bowling, and Fielding: the Laws of Cricket, Match-playing, Single-wicket, &c. &c. By AN OLD CRICKETER.

THE BOAT; AND HOW TO MANAGE IT. By SALACIA.

BAILY BROTHERS, CORNHILL.

Second Edition, Foolscap Octavo, Price 5s.,

THE GAMEKEEPER'S DIRECTORY;

CONTAINING INSTRUCTIONS FOR THE

Preservation of Game, Destruction of Vermin, and the Prevention of Poaching, &c. &c.

By J. B. JOHNSON,

AUTHOR OF "THE SPORTSMAN'S CYCLOPÆDIA," "SHOOTER'S COMPANION," &C.

W. KENT AND CO., PATERNOSTER ROW.

BAILY'S SERIES OF WINNERS,

From Paintings by J. F. Herring, sen., and Harry Hall.

Beautifully coloured, Price £1. 1s. each.

No. 1. Beeswing	No. 24. Surplice
No. 2. Charles XII	No. 25. Flying Dutchman
No. 3. Cotherstone	No. 26. Voltigeur
No. 4. Poison	No. 27. Canezou
No. 5. Nutwith	No. 28. Teddington
No. 6. Confidence	No. 29. Nancy
No. 7. Alice Hawthorn	No. 30. Newminster
No. 8. Orlando	No. 31. Daniel O'Rourke
No. 9. Princess	No. 32. Stockwell
No. 10. Foigh-a-Ballagh	No. 33. West Australian
No. 11. Merry Monarch	No. 34. Irish Birdcatcher
No. 12. The Emperor	No. 35. Melbourne
No. 13. The Baron	No. 36. Andover
No. 14. Sweetmeat	No. 37. Kt. of St. George
No. 15. Pyrrhus the First	No. 38. Virago
No. 16. Mendicant	No. 39. Wild Dayrell
No. 17. Alarm	No. 40. Rataplan
No. 18. Slane	No. 41. Ellington
No. 19. Gladiator	No. 42. Blink Bonny
No. 20. Sir Tatton Sykes	No. 43. Beadsman
No, 21. Cossack	No. 44. Musjiid
No. 22. Van Tromp	No. 45. Thormanby
No. 23. The Hero	No. 46. St. Albans.

London :—BAILY BROTHERS, CORNHILL.

12-

www.ingramcontent.com/pod-product-compliance
Lightning Source LLC
Chambersburg PA
CBHW020356100426

42812CB00001B/77